Incomplete Texts

Mohammed Y. Burhan

Translated from Arabic into English by:
Maan Burhan

Order this book online at www.trafford.com
or email orders@trafford.com

Most Trafford titles are also available at major online book retailers.

Printed in the United States of America.

ISBN: 978-1-4269-6214-1 (sc)
ISBN: 978-1-4269-6256-1 (hc)
ISBN: 978-1-4269-6257-8 (e)

Library of Congress Control Number: 2011904427

Trafford rev. 03/24/2011

 www.trafford.com

North America & international
toll-free: 1 888 232 4444 (USA & Canada)
phone: 250 383 6864 ◆ fax: 812 355 4082

Spears in the old image

The Story Of Creation

With one finger
In the overflowing water,
A circle had He drawn.
With two hands, therein
Man had He drown!

---

* that may be so, because life is an act of drowning ;
all the legends of creation start like a god playing with
water.

Disappointment

Sixty years ago
Maybe over,
I gave him birth.
I crowned him with a new name.
A man I made of him,
A nearby brother,
With my jugular vein
He lived together.
Sixty years never apart;
My son "Dream",
I slaughtered him
Nearby the window the other day
Having become old,
Not true!

A Wish

A moon of flour
And stars of sesame,
It is the sky to the hungry.
A loaf of bread... Not more!

Drowned

With my only-left-waterless hand,
I long waved to you
At which you only raised your hands!
Were you waving back?

Thirst

Fed up with food and flowers are we
With TV screens.
Fed up even with our
Dead-like miens at the mirrors..
Where to end up?
Water. Where is water!

Just If

Had time been money
All spent would it be
Waiting to see her face!

Siblings

Europe whose whiteness
Unburdened her to surrender
And Africa whose blackness
Pitied her not to burn
Blessed is defeat ... a home for all.

Passion

When her golden earring
Tore my palm,
My blood wept,
White... transparent
Like tears

Wait

Your black gown
Goes much like my lone night.
Why not open at the middle
To light up my days!

Weep

I gifted the sea with a flower
That once was yours.
I shed it into the water
Why, the moon fell
And my feet sobbed
Over the sand…

Lust

She slept with me the whole night
Flapped upon my chest like a partridge
While our clothes,
Aside on the bed
And naked of us,
Were shyly picking each other up!

The Truth

A woman never comes close
For more tenderness to give,
Rather, to smell more
How sick you are of her!

Panting

Another day passes by,
And over the hands of the clock,
It pours forth light
To bite parts off our dreams
Then to fade
Even before
We open our arms
To welcome!

Sacrilege

The moon,
It is a hole in the dress of night.
The morning is...
The night's public hot flesh!

Paradox

Cries
Whenever in need to
Smile

Zabadani

Ever since the apple
Became the source of sin,
For planting apples
Famous my village has been!

Toil

As it every day pays
      For getting there,
           The ladder is the only
                  To hate peaks

Endurance

Whenever I hold my pen,
I picture Moses
Breaking his stick
Kissing Pharaoh's hand
Then shouts at me:
You are drowning
Along with your poems.

Renewal

I escort the poem
To the wide-open door of glitter
Then... again...
Back to life
An incomplete text that
A poem might once
Draw accomplished.

Distance Grasp

Here, beside me, lies he
Stunned at the waiting death are we,
Yet still makes mock of me:
"Envy me O river
I get there, no suffer."

A wry smile I give, in secret
And make sure that he not reach it;

"He whose eagerness to reach be untried
Will reach with his rapture aside."

Publishing

My poem
Leaves betrayed of me
When with silence it reacts
To the love of the others...

Glow

I dress my silence up
To out-sight the angel of death

Alas, my smell betrays me:
Whatever I do…
I smell of death.

Prophecy

A loner
A failure rebel
Yet still obstinate,

I shall always butt this rock
Till the ever dwelling grief
In my head
Departs
Or else
I better die for it.

The Truth

A bit of a heretic
Makes God practise being in rapture
More than a clan of believers, do or picture.

The Hospital of Condolence

When too much pain
Is all you gain,
Never envy the others
For having less bothers.
Think it over and over again
And recall pain itself as main
Can you stand all that it suffers?

Dubiousness

No,
The Christ was not
On the cross
I did see Him
He was holding the cross fast
On his back...

Death "To Wasim"

Twenty-five years
A clown- like
Dancing on the very edge of life...
Now... Just now
To the bed of your tomb
…… Get down
And breathe up!

Death Struggle

A statue inside each
Longs to find his niche,
Longs to be inactant
So why are we so hesitant?
We go; we come and wait
And often we get so late,
So late, so late, so late,
To becoming a corpse in state.

Signboard

On the gate of life
And one on the afterlife
A sign would save the strife:
We are not responsible and never care
For losing your hopes or feeling despair.

Doomsday

Rapt as if God passed by him
And with the eager left,
So celebrately,
Raphael smiles…
Eventually he is sounding the trumpet!
A lone task
That cost a humanity to wait.

The Poem of Insomnia

The Gray Female Departure

You strike my sadness
As a crowned bride.
Out of my gloomy orchard
You pick up lilies
And read me stories
About lovers.

From a window
Outlooking the sea,
You gather the stars to me
Along with the fishermen songs.

You drop, the gown of the dense night
On my trembling shoulder.

Are you part of me so that I feel
Your agony dwelling my ribs?

Am I part of you so that I come to life
Every time you say, "good morning"?
O, woman, who spreads over my poem
Like meanings do,
I wish you lent me your voice
As speech no longer gets me.
It is your indifference that
Key secrets my death.

I wish you lent me your blood
So that I grow,
In the veins of those
Ever heading for sunrise,
A home that gives them back
Where they had cried.

That is… how ….you always do.
You strike my sadness
As a crowned bride,
Treading my wheat and voice:
Slowly my princess … haste not
My heart is clutching
At that train of your dress.

The Incomplete Crime

Half close the door for my absence,
Let not open of it!
Night will get in
So will neat men do
After you.

Foolish questions will they thrust
Into my wounds
And look, among the bags set,
For an overtaking death.

They will read a poem
I am already rid of

That is what they always do
Shear off the truth in the neck
To deeply scrutinize in light

O Gentlemen,
Be kind to my things,
I still have a living song
In the haziness of time
It is not yet dead.
I still have an old speech
Hung over the wall

An old sweater
With sleeves out
For stay ups.
Some cigarette stubs
Like stabs
Planted over the dump.

Nay, gentlemen
Sail not in a stain
Hanged under the pillow!
Ink is no blood
Nor my fingers daggers.

At the middle of time
After it be put out
They will leave,
When I rise up
Out of my own heap
To rearrange my ribs,
And to bestow death a truce
So that it, of my corpse
And the chaos they left,
Takes a rest.

So then, half close the door
And sweep your voice
Off the air in the room.
Let not your white gloves
Stretch over my blood
Like a prostitute!
It is a pity
To mark your crime
As incomplete!

Loss

One day you will get to know
That it is not the blossoms that resemble me.
And that the ninth tumbler is my father
Who brought me up to heartache and cry.

One day you will get to know
That my chest,
Whose manliness you drank,
Would no more shelter
Your little fragile bird
That fears the tenderest breeze.

Nor upon my chest you more can wilt
Transparent like a tear.

It may be life that shall, one day,
Teach you
How to perfect
The loss
Of the others…

Truce

Light is the news this evening.
So coquettish sounds the reporter,
Having worn her femininity,
Replacing the helmet
With a white rose on the hair.

How female would she be
When unequipped with war!

Chaste is the news this evening,
Less murder,
Less is our blood in the barricades,
Low the crown of the rapid death.

Blind is the news this evening
Come on love
Let me snipe your lips
With a brief kiss
Before the raids
Of breaking news!

It is Damascus

A face that slaps the roads
And a sweetheart,
Whose scarf on a bench of absence,
She forgot.

And trees stretching high,
But no close to God
As out of reach is the sky.

Some peanuts between two glasses
An ashtray for memory and cigarettes…
It is Damascus then!
A poem that unveils her loincloth,
To prostitute herself

At the face of her ever raped poet:
Barada
Deflower me wherever you wish.
Stretch me a tight string
To your arch of disappointment
And leave my socks to the wind
That will hang high the flag for you.

Barada! O male river
Penetrate my mud like a wedge
And pour your dark milk out
Over my navel
So that the world restarts again
Out of this point...

The Spacious

On your way to her face
You all march forth,
Lightly and heavily
Dressed in your silence
And burdened with the questions,
Looking into the mirrors
For a pain like yourselves.
This is you…
This is what you always do:
Since the break out of creation
You carouse in the merge of a woman
Pawned to phantom.
While I…
Whom God created of tears and depress
Overpass your roads.

I lay ropes over the trees
And dance above your funeral:
I am the one to have cut the hand of Venus
I am the one to have slaughtered Astarte the cruel.

Nay, statues are you all
And the loss of yours, I foresee
All …. You … Who
Ramble on the boundaries
Of an expansive woman.

The Caller

She left the constellation of the firmament
Why the night that moment dwelt.
From the hole of the key would she enter,
Forests and horses soon came after.
Out of her navel, stars she hanged in the room's air.
Over my body, she, her hair, then passed
That was when my blood had shined.
She frisked my pillows for dreams like her.

She paged through my papers
For words, she thought, of hers.
All my clothes she threw into disorder,
For a smell of a woman that might be there.
When all she found was naught,
She stole my sleep and went out.
Over my bedsheet, she left a mare,
And a moon on the words over there.
Colorful trees on my lime-green shirt,
She those had also left:
The poem of insomnia loves me
So jealous for me she seems she be.

Pagan Tale

Twenty cigarettes, after which we had lain,
I and she, out of the loop, out of pain.
A year each of us was, long, long ago
Tales about ancient peoples, we were so.
 We exchanged the faces of the wind
Over that tight and narrow bed.
She, over me, sailed north,
To her lands, I went far south.
I deep reveled in the pine
Sinking so deep in her wine.
Then she sobbed with tears,
Blowing out all her fears,
Blowing out all her wonders:
Oh, my dear where are your fingers?
An arrow in the back street of my head
Raced, looking for a victim straight ahead.
O Noah: where are my fingers?
She is asking! Fulfill her wonders.
Collect not the sky of water ahead,
Nor plow through the torrents of God,
Without even looking behind
Here I am, so alone, so aside.

I am still preparing the winds
And casting all I can, of spells
So that God, the ship protects.
Noah, you the prophet of waves
Your blood mystically runs through my veins.
When you asked me to be you,
And that took place as if on cue.
This was for nothing, but out of purity,
I shall, thus, never show disloyalty.
And from my complaint
I shall be restrained.
And for the mighty prophecy of yours
Shall I build up a temple for waters.
Here are all the trees of mine
I burnt them all for the hands of thine.
I picked up out of its leaves
Places, for survival, and seats.

Why discard me and all my silver?
Does my shadow look much higher
Than that shadow of your ship?
Then I shall kill and even snip.

Or I might gift
Half of it
For those who go
Without a single shadow.
Just take me with you, take me
For who, without a sun, shall you be?
A sun of my speech in your sky,
That makes your sun and sky that high?
And who, without my dreams, shall you be?
I have always been with you, and you with me.
I have always sweated over your timber,
The milky wishes of mine in whisper.
Your reckless nails still moan inside my head,
And that reddish rust over them is my blood.
Why, then, go far without me?
Why discard me and all my silver in the sea?

She shook my shoulder while sobbing
She rather shook so hard for asking:
So they left you! Had they done?

I had no mate, why without me
                           The ship had gone.

Intimate Companionship

Over the choppy river,
With an envy flavor,
The tree throws a handful
                Of a flower:
If I had his spirit, the restless,
All the plains would I embrace.
Over the peaks would I have drawn
A scented sketch of a crown.

In his secret, with the rambling sound
The river says with his voice bound:
"Just if, I, my shadow found,
Like a tree would I stand erect
Only then would I have a rest."

The chemistry of happiness

Do not seize life
With struggle and strife.
Let pass of it
Without even a greet
Like a woman, a stranger,
We only wish we capture.
Among all things, the prettier
Leave in our memory a flower.

Do not seize delight
O beast, O hurt
Your prey is prettier before
It is eaten and killed, far more,
Spend your time just watching
Behind that wall of timing
Pray for the wheat for the smell
Of the rain over there where you dwell.
Share with the whisper of the wind
The delightful weddings that had passed.
Nations told nations and their speech spread
That the earth is round like a loaf of bread;

And that crying, like laughter,
Is a moment following the other.

Do not set a trap for happiness.
Wise would Adam have been
If he just
   Waited
for the apple
   To fall !...
Just
   if .....

Strangers

Here, we strangers, in the faraway lands
Wave for time with our poor hands.
We, our tobacco, generously give
For the by-passers who never here live.
We sip the hunger of the heart
On the very benches of the wait.
Truth has held some dizziness
That befalls our souls and heads.
A stranger is born a stranger
In the winds and lands of danger.
He sings on, on and on
For the memories that all have gone.
He dances round the lastest of his candles
With mere words, the dying soul he handles.

He is like the obstinate swans
To death, through the doors of joy, he runs.

Fall has the ever-bewailing leaves
The pallor of seasons is all we seize.
How much agony feeling must come
Before of names we all have become?
Names that would one time with raring
Remind us of our being and meaning.
We strangers in the faraway lands,
In the winds and everlasting exiles
We sing for memory and dance for swans.

We shout at the faces of all the prophets
Is there no such holy scriptures,
That might one day fall and guide us?

O you panel of quick death,
On this very and same earth.
Had the road had legs been done
So fast to reach would it have gone.
If the rain had got a face,
It would have shined with all its grace.
If the river had got a mouth,
It would have kissed the sea at the mouth.
Oh… if only we are the same,
Nay, we never this can claim:
That we are same in the pleasures
Of inhaling and exhaling
That we are same in the desires
For the trees and birds nor in loving.
Nay, we are never the same the moments we die;
We eagerly wait for good death, to which we fly,
While, for the sake of your life, you always pray.

He told them

He told them: I will be born in hours
In a night or maybe in less than days
So prepare the pots and all the cloths.
Well boil the water with ginger and cinnamon
Be well prepared for my coming, you come on.
Don't miss covering my cotton bed
With ambergris and opium to lay my head
For I, nine long boring months, have lead.

He knows well that this was what he said,
But knows not what that moment had happened.

When a thread of light broke over his head
From his legs two rough hands, him had pulled.
His body then the dust had felt ,
Dust where thorns and ants dwelt.

He looked up then, bleary-eyed
To the thighs that were really wide
A woman undressed to her belly
Wrapped him with a rag so shoddy

She threw him to
        A wood cart
            That soon
                And slowly
                Rolled

                        Toward
                        The valley
            of life.

Things of a crying grief

A gravestone

It is not death the painful, it is rather to be the last to die... it is to watch the stars of the story falling one after another out of pain.

How adroit was Nietzsche when he waited for the "superman" to come to being in that legend of his, and how poor was he when he gave little notice to the end of the story! When he did not perceive that the end of this feverish race would come to a gruff announcement on a gravestone...

He deeply thought about this while eagerly watching the evening newscast. He never cared for peace or war in this world. Nor was he attracted by the courtesy cold kisses on TV screens. He, however, used to sit pinned before that luminous box at this very exact time, to do nothing but look for some gestures that might look like him among the corpses that the world news abounds with.

He was fond of raising his glance slowly to his gestures during the tranquility of his soul.... He, moreover, was madly in love with observing his coming death.

Eighty years ago, maybe over, when his mother died, he wept bitterly for her... but then he had such a relieving idea!

He thought to himself, "What if man had the will to determine the timing of his death, forty years for example? There would then be no space for pain and disappointment as long as the end is well known."

He cried less when his brother passed away, and it was then when he built two gravestones, one of which was his.

Something inspiring told him that forty was the appropriate age for death and that he had to be well prepared long before that.

In his fifty-five, he was that agonized at the death of his wife whom he loved far more than life. Back from the funeral and without shedding a single tear, he returned too fatigued.

While he was puffing smoke along with disappointment out of his number ninety cigarette, he held a wide black pen and over his gravestone, he penned:

"In the name of God, Most gracious Most Merciful: O you the one in complete rest and satisfaction! Come back to Your Lord, well-pleased and well pleasing unto him! Enter you, then, among my honored slaves, and enter you My Paradise!"...

He was so happy with the words "complete rest and satisfaction" and with "well-pleasing". He confidently realized that that sixty-five was not the average age for death; it rather was the utmost age for life in most countries in the world. He sought to ascertain that in a clipping of a newspaper, which he had hidden in a book twenty years ago.

In his eighty-seven, he was laughing to death when some young people were casting his son's corpse in the gap of a tomb, why people thought he was demented.

The truth was that he was thinking of that wretched boy whom he thought he would protect him from the last attack of death; when he was calmly swinging over the shoulders of the escorts...

That day he returned home and added his name on the gravestone preceded by the phrase "Here lies". He also remembered that his grandmother lived for fifty-nine years:

Oh... Are the coming years enough to get prepared?

He, anyway, will try to make them be so.

Today it is his tenth year after one hundred, and he has just come back from a funeral of some neighboring child who has been run over in an awful accident on his way back from school.

The newscaster apologized for postponing the newscast, to invite the viewers to watching an important football game...

He got up to the TV and muted it, pushing a button in its chest, then went to the gravestone... He held the black pen... and ... after the words "He died in ..." he, between parentheses, added: (still waiting).

The wall

(1)

As if a cop had been killed or that the mayor had had the fifth heart attack, we woke up that dawn at the loud wailings of our women, which brought about the dispersion of our usual sluggish rouse.

It is strange how our wives become so cognizant of the calamities of the night before we do. Although we spend the longest part of it playing together those exhausting plays of the dark, they sneak off the beds with the very approach of the dawn more active and vivid while we get that decline in vigor like the dead-beat oxen after a long cultivation day.

We woke up, horrified, and jumped out of our beds to the thresholds of our dusty allies to witness our wives stretching down the ground, as if down the funeral cloth, hitting against their chests, scandalously showing their reddish breasts that looked like the hot loaves of the morning.

None of us looked for his own two loaves of bread, as we thought that something grave must have happened:

Someone pissed on the wall...

Wish we sank down the earth or that the sky fell over our heads, better than hearing such misfortune: Did someone really do it?

We rushed west the town, dark-faced with our fear outrunning us, and followed by the sinister fate, which we realized it was inevitable if true was what we heard.

(2)

Is it a wall in a magnificent mansion? Is it part of a great wall of a city, where people slept full and thirst-quenched?

Had it ever been a lofty dam in a land, which God showered with water and life?

We do not know and do not even care; it is more than sufficient for us that it has always erected as a symbol for something so powerful that kept evil and harm away, and brought us happiness and relief.

We do respect it as our fathers and grandfathers did. None of us even complained about its being an obstacle that had always prevented us from reaching the stream of water. Its presence even doubled the distance to get to water and forced our wives to take the mountain path, which took them the whole daylong to fill the jars. When they finally came back, blood-legged, thanks to the thorns and stones on the way, we used to forgive them to expressing their pain by moaning too long, and some stern faces was all we could make.

The mayor… oh mayor … how much he loved that wall! Even more than he loved his own children; he always told us that God prevented us from rain and greenness, that He afflicted us with poverty, weakness and being belittled by the others, but God gave us what was far better:

He bestowed that wall upon us out of being so graceful! We should preserve it so that it never ceases to exist.

One year, out of many others, and as unusual, the sky rained copiously. "A year", said my grandma, "we never had witnessed before."

It rained all the days and nights that we were so pleased in the beginning that our crops would be well irrigated and that our soil would be saturated with fertility. We even did not complain when the wall debarred water from being out of it. Then, however, our lands were flooded and our little corps perished, to let us live a year more austere than those of drought.

In spite of all, we always repeated what our mayor taught us:

"Our crops are destroyed, our houses are so too, but we always praise You, for Your kindness as You protected our wall from the tyranny of Your water, as You kept it for us that lofty to remind us with Your mercy."

(3)

(Someone pissed on the wall…)

We came to the place seeking the protection of God to find the mayor in a deplorable condition. He had thrown himself down to earth holding his head with both hands and wailing like women over the adversity that he would never get over.

Wish we sank down the earth or that the sky fell over our heads before we saw that damp spot spreading like oil does on a piece of paper.

The catastrophe tongue-tied us all and paralyzed us to fall down, one by another like those targets in a death camp.

Our tears gave us no succor as our eyes were still suffering from that drought caused by our "early wake-up". Those terrifying moments we lived dehydrated our bodies but from those drops of… that found a way out of our trembling and shaking bodies through our pants.

Hard times passed before that trembling voice of salvation shouted out:

It might be water!

Getting his head out of his hands as if he was unsheathing a sword longing for blood, our mayor suspiciously gazed into our faces and hurried to that spot, the closest to his face was then the wall as he was smelling and even licking as if living a dream that soon turned into a nightmare. It was then when he got up with the force of the disappointment sending him reeling against the wall, widely open-handed:

Woe is me… It is urine ….

He then cried on:

We are made an aim.

We bent our heads in distress:

Be kind to our feelings mayor! Who might want to harm us? Our barren lands are even no home for insects, our sky is sterile and our women are stall-fed fat cows of whom we made undesirable to capture.

We looked upward to the sky, we dreamt of clouds passing and green plains running like deer, we dreamt of springs flowing in streams between the houses and of women like nymphs dressed in white silk dresses carrying jars of water and honey and waiting for us.

The mayor then realized very well that he made the wrong guesswork. He, therefore, changed his expectations fearing that we sink deeper in our dreams, which he examined for so long:

(No one dares to do this but a mad man…).

That was very true. Who dares to trespass on the sacred wall? He must be a gawky long-legged mad man who never can guess where his wicked deeds would lead. Who might dishonor our relief? Who might make a toy of our peace and stability? He must be such an idiot who will have what we will, of curse and bad destiny.

As our town knew but one brainless, Saadoon, all our accusations were leveled against him. He was leaning somewhere close to us and laughing loud. It was the first time then when we felt how sarcastic and scornful he was.

Without a prior notice, three men headed to Saadoon, one of them hit him on the shoulder then on the legs by a cudgel while the other two men dragged him to where the mayor was standing.

We ringed the men fearfully, waiting for what we still had to imagine!

The Mayor shouted at Sadoon

What bad consequences your misdeed would drive, you idiot! I have always feared such a reckless deed of yours, but... I ... never expected you would commit such a crime to your town ... to the people who sustained your madness and opened their arms to care and feel for you.

Saadoon now had lost his sarcastic face that turned into a pale leaf, so ready to fall.

The mayor uttered no word, but his looks did. Those looks that eyed us beggarly ... he then decided something:

"I will decide nothing about you". He sent a provocative spark out of his eyes.

"Here is the felon, right before you… soiling your wall… it is a curse that nothing better than reprisal can ward off. Do what you think is true".

Speechlessness hit us for a moment, why we, for a moment, kept silent… we saw thunders hitting our houses down to earth and turning dust into ash, and birds in flocks striking their fiery stones over our heads. We pictured our wives coquettishly lying on the beds of the strangers. We also pictured our dear mayor wrapped with a white coffin and being received by purple worms in the dark hole of the grave.

All the devils of fear ran on our legs toward Saadoon. We were one mass… we smashed his little head with our feet, and with our hands we cut his body into pieces. We did this altogether as if we were praying in a group in the morning of the Eid. Nothing of his gestures could tell who he was. His hot blood irrigated the thirsty land to the last drop.

When the wedge of fear was now loose, we hung our eyes on the sky. There were no thunders; it, rather, was the sun getting hotter. There were no swimming birds in the space; they were swarms of flies hovering over our heads and looking for their share of the prey. Far there, we saw our wives with no one following them:

O… Our Lord…. We are saved…

We slept peacefully that night. We were sure that nothing harmful would be done to us as we punished the guilty.

We, however, slept thirsty that night as what had happened during the day and the din that followed caused our wives to forget their journey to the water spring, especially that, as you may know now, the wall makes double of the distance to water...

We slept filled with the joy of salvation... and with a tacit envy for the nearby town, whose people sleep quenched, as they have no wall.

Curtains

Alia is as clear as a white cloud, as innocent as a bird's singing whose heart is a wide sea and whose voice is a sky…

The city around which were trees and flowers was dead now, and people put on weary eyes whose wings were broken… but she still has two golden wings through which she flies faraway beyond the plains and beyond the mountains.

Alia hasn't learnt how to die yet, she still thinks that the grave is a garden whose white stones are but flowers.

When the sun was sluggishly and lazily collecting its shiny luggage, Alia glanced at it begging (Stay a little bit longer, I do not like the night). The sun, however, took little notice to that childish invocation and thus continued its work so bored and tired as it spent the whole day dreadfully watching the town and illuminating the ragged faces of people that looked like yellow pages in old books.

Alia sits in an outlying corner in the courtyard counting her fingers, one, two, three, …., eight, then she stops as she can no more see her two other fingers, as her father told her once:

"I'll cut them off if you try to hold the pencil"

Science is light. This was written in red letters on the wall of the school, and she likes the sun.

Her elder brother said:

"You're not going to school; Sheikh Sayed's daughter learnt nothing from school but writing letters to the boys."

Her mother told her off when she saw her playing with Yusuf and Khalid. She then pushed her hard and said:

"Boys play with boys, while girls stand in the kitchen beside their mothers to learn how to wash dishes…."

Alia went back to counting, one, two… eight.

She every day watches her mates running joyfully with their papers and pencils and repeating loudly some school songs and chants.

The father says to the mother:

"I told you a thousand times girls are not to learn". She will go to school, just because she likes to chant!.

Alia counts, one, two, eight, … nine, ten..

Paper bags scattered on both sides of the stark road that looks like a deserted port that has been so for two falls.

Alia collects as much bags as she can to make a notebook, and makes a pencil of a cold piece of coal.

Hope is an angel with a tail that the desperate try to grasp…

The window of the class looked like a wide horizon to the gold-winged eyes that were gazing from behind.

Alia learns more and more as she, every day, watches the teacher, stares at the board, and writes down on her brown paper that looked so dark as if cultivated.

She now knows how to write, but no longer remembers the neighboring boy…

The father asks:

"And where does Alia go every morning?"

The mother replies: "She goes out to pasture the cattle."

The days fell one by another, each day, each hour, looked like a festival with its children and new clothes.

One cesarean-born day that Alia felt as if it were a childish old man refusing to walk, in spite of the two legs and the crutch he had, the parents shouted at the headmaster during a meeting with him:

It is too hot a sun and our children no more can stand it, they are all complaining about the sun striking through the window.

In that meeting Salim, the tailor, said, "I can help solve this."

Thus, the death-colored purple cloud veiled the transparency of the horizon of that window, what made Alia go back bow-headed with her yellow pale paper like a doleful moon. Back to the kitchen and to learning how to clean dishes. No more golden wings in her eyes to fly faraway beyond the plains and the mountains; Alia is now a young girl at the age of the broken lilies. She hates the sun and only counts to ten.

Lira

She came out of the bathroom, wrapped in his soft velvet shirt after being lazy to open her traveling cases that were lying down one of the corners in the room.

She threw her shadow that smelled off soap, over his face and started to rub her hair with the new towel.

The short shirt gave a sonorous hooray above the two white thighs every time her hand went through the locks of her wet hair that ran over her back like a stream of thirst.

Oh… How surprised he was at her presence… he is sitting now on the verge of the bed, at the edge of his silence, gnawing on his amazement and trying to believe something. Something that was as impossible as a gray-haired crow.

As she turned putting the towel on a nearby chair, her body seemed so overwhelmed with presence. What was happening could no longer be denied.

A wicked desire raided him to swoop on her waist to shake it hard so that her long absence falls down the edges of his memory.

However, instead of doing that, he let his eyes go after a drop of water that was making her way out of her hair to fall on her white leg, drawing a thin transparent line that looked like that of a story…

Who said that the body of women is to read from the front?

Women can be read from all the sides, they rather can be more profoundly read from behind, or maybe in a larger scale of lust.

He did not believe her calling sound was around, telling him she was coming and asking him to meet her in a specific place… He thought it was a lie or a put on, but her voice was confident and full of truth.

This is no longer important now; what really matters is how would this end up? Where will that red line be drawn to stop this congestion?

Here she stands before him filling the air with the smell of the Damascene bitter orange and drawing a begging smile on her face:

I am hungry…

Is Damascus so far? How many lies must he give to the dreams before getting to it?

The picture of the absent city climbed up his mind and, out of the blue, he got up shivering. He recovered his consciousness to find her moaning painfully between his heavy hands that were wringing her embraced.

He never felt that he loved her. It was like a game, like a childish passion. Each of us must have started his course of love at the neighboring window.

However, it is different now; she is no longer the old Suha, his neighbor. She is now something like the streets, like the houses there; it is something like the slumbering pain there in the convolutions of the mind... or it might be like a bygone poem whose opening is the only thing that he still has in mind.

I swear I am hungry... you know? I have got no bite to eat since the early morning as I have no one Mark. All I have is few thousand Liras that you will have to help me exchange tomorrow.

How youthful you are O brunette woman who wears his memory and dark shirt! How lustrous while carousing over the furniture where forlornness had long dwelt!

Come on ... stretch out your half-naked hand on the table... rub yourself against his low chair. Over his books that are put up like a coffin, strew your hair that drips water and thirst.

From now on, all these things he one day thought to be so little and trivial will dwell the mornings of Damascus... The travelling voice of Fayrooz in the wrinkles of the coffee will be having a new foam that will be like a greeting, a terse one given by the city that he gave love when in return it killed him:

Oh... I am tired.

She threw her back against that of the chair's for relaxation, and for the cries to become louder at the thighs, hammering heavily over his head nailing out pain and memories.

She was so vivid that day, when they were all alone in that room against the kitchen. They were young then, playing (heads or tails). Her body was not that ripe yet, there were, however, some slight changes taking place and leaving him to his fear and surprise. The body he used to wrap while playing hide-and-seek had more complex elevations now especially at the breast and ones up the pelvis. He, moreover, heard a strange panting every time he touched a new place of her body.

She held the coin closing her two hands tightly:

So now... heads or tails?

Mmm.... tails.

The foxy girl surprised him when she buried the coin in her body and looked wickedly at him. He was so young to understand what her smile meant, so he inserted his hand in her dress asking for his coin. Nothing but a mighty slap on his face could deter him from looking for his coin. He came to on the screams of his mother reproaching him angrily and asking Suha to go back home as it was too late.

He began to wipe off the wet ring around her eyes. At the top of her cold nose, he groped for the redness of an alley he used to go into at the break of the morning coming back from the café or out of a recent advent of love.

She then did not cringe away from his trembling hand, but rather closed her eyes in a lustful collusion, breathing out intermittently ... odorously; he knew the sky would open up this night and that some death would give out his first scream of life when the story comes to an end.

"I miss you" ... she said... she tied her hands and laid her head on one shoulder being shy to say so. Her neck glittered as a river of light when her shirt ebbed uncovering the other shoulder.

He was no longer able to cease the moment and imprison it in between both of them, what made an old image fall down his memory; it flared before his eyes like those dying flashes in a wrecked lighthouse.

He recalled Lolo, the prostitute, whom his friends hired that night and queued at the door to go in one by the other.

When it was his turn, he came in to find her lying on her front giving out so hot a panting. He no longer remembers how things went on... he found himself tenderly and painfully touching her hair when she cried out: "bring in the next, this one is dead"... Nothing upset him then, as he had not even taken any of his clothes off. He gave a wry pale smile to his friend's wondering eyes. He went out to the streets of the sleeping city crying or maybe laughing, he cannot exactly remember... or it is no longer something important to exert an effort to call to mind.

Woe ... you brunette woman who puts on his memory and dark shirt... what do you expect him to say? He misses you? Well, he does!

Geography sometimes conspires as well; the flocks of swallow heading there committed a suicide in the middle of the way, as it was a long way to Damascus.

So now, get up quench his thirst that coffins him... it is not a treason to present him with the key of the city that is hidden in the warm cache in your skin.

Who said that the body of women is to read from behind?

A woman can be read through her blood and the trained cavalier can recreate and reshape bodies as the intelligent reader can write the one text many times.

He snatched her out of his blood and away from her chair... throwing her over the bed like a fragment of a broken country. He tore his velvet shirt and the remains of her astonishment to start snapping her dark skin looking for a missing Lira!

Kite

(1)

I do swear I had never seen one like it before. Nor had my father bought me one to recognize it or even to match such a thing with a name in my mind. That is why, when I heard the teacher asking us to draw a kite, I got so panicked.

That was my first day at school when the teacher cried, after making sure that each of the students had his paper and pencil on the table:

"Draw this kite"

He held the chalk in his long fingers to sketch on that endless green surface, some lines that raised nothing to my mind. Then, he irritably threw the chalk, and began to walk round the desks.

I was lost in the middle of that wide, white and measureless page. When I held the pencil, a sudden feeling of loneliness came over me. Her picture jumped before my eyes when she sharpened the pencil and smiled to have put the apple in my bag this morning. I also realized how far my mother was now.

Yes, it was my first day at school. I did not know then why I took a nap. Was it out of the deep grief or because I was still sleepy? I do not know. All I know is that a harsh poke in my head made me wake up.

How tall that teacher was! He cried out:

"Sleeping? You drew nothing, huh?"

I tried to untie my tied tongue to say something, why I looked so foolish. He took the initiative with a powerful slap on my face:

Whose son are you?

I tried to remember what my sister had taught me that evening but in vain:

I am … I am…

He replied hatefully:

Draw on...

Ever since that day I cannot even draw three cross lines, the hysteria of kites and the sharpened pencils do grip me.

(2)

My mid sister's return from Saudi Arabia is considered booty to us, we little brothers. Her return was as joyful to us as the last day of school and as remunerative as the feast days. We spend long nights before the big day dreaming of the surprises the big green case might hold.

That afternoon, all the female relatives along with those of the neighbors swarmed in our house to cheerfully receive my sister...

Talks and noise was all what we gave no ear to as we were stealing the looks at the other room where that green case had that crown of eager and wait. We were so fed up with the gossips that seemed endless, waiting that moment they leave us to our dear booty.

Finally, after the boring wait, here comes the long waited call:

Come on boys and girls...

We lagged behind pretending to be shy with our hearts jumping impatiently to gather round the case that was now laid in the middle of the room like an appetizing banquet:

The angel-like hand of my sister starts to distribute the gift:

This new red car is Salim's... this little dancing and singing bride is Nuha's... this rifle that fires colorful water is Khalid's...

Then after a short silence while looking for something at the bottom of the case, she looked at me drawing a cute smile on her face, which made my heart jump out:

This blue kite is yours... she pushed it before my face as she carried it on her palms like a dead silent body of a child:

To my surprise I stepped back fearfully:

What is wrong with you? It is cute, isn't it?

You will fly it high over the roof up there.

I stepped forward pale and trembling... it was the first time when I saw it closely... I turned it over carefully and laid it aside without getting it out of its bag.

I cannot count how many days passed before my brothers got it out to fly joyfully in the sky up the roof while I watched them even unable to go close to them.

(3)

When your son starts a new phase in his life means that you too are making a good headway in your sacred social turn. I was thinking about this when my wife was busy hanging the balloons and decorating, having prepared the bright dishes of food and sweets on the table.

Today is the first day for our son, Qasim, in school. We have prepared a small party and invited our relatives and some neighbors.

My wife is greatly stuck to the criteria of the new methods of education. She says we have to make our son understand the importance of this day in which he opens a new phase in his life. She says that the positive impression we provide him with will be a motive for him to enable him to work on harder during the coming school life.

I could add nothing to what seemed to be that logical as her thought betrayed a very advanced educational mentality.

I sat aside interestingly watching the eager movements around, and listening to the chatters about the memories of the early days in school… my eyes were moving from the hands of the clock to my wife's face that shined increasingly with the progress of the time.

It is half past one, the bell rang … we all got up and my wife's eagerness pushed her to the door.

A moment of disappointment roamed the room when we, from behind, could notice the cheerful gestures of my wife collapsing down out of shock.

Few other moments of silence preceded the movement of my wife making way to Qasim who was gloomily coming in with his face shining off pain.

As if he didn't notice the others, he headed straight to me.

The more he came close the more the overflowing grief over his face screamed out… I started to become more certain of a slap of long fingers that left behind a red octopus over the smooth skin.

One step far, he stopped, looked up at my face and with a blaming voice:

Dad, why didn't you buy me a kite before?

Out of the two small eyes, two large drops of dew severely fell over the new school uniform.

The bolt

(1)

He pushes the bolt with his hand – oh – how tired he is today... he leans on the edge of the callous bed in the have-nothing-much inside room, and then he stoops down and gets engrossed to untie the ragged laces of his green shoes.

How much time might he need to dream?

How much dark does he need to sleep?

He throws his back to the bed, opens wide his mouth giving a long foolish yawn and closing his eyelids trapping inside the pleasures of the ever dwelling phantom of his girl. Harmonious full breasts … round black eyes … and a hot cylindrical torso … that takes different shapes every time it tightens and releases with every inhale and exhale… svelte long hair … rosy lips that he pleases to play with, so savagely… uh.. How delicious! He tosses aside to the right when the image of Husnieh, the greengrocer's daughter, flashes in his memory when they parted beyond the old ruin. She said then that he still had to grow much older to gain the full mastery of where to touch the female… she is so stupid, so cold… she doesn't know that if she slept with his imagination just for one day, she would be more satisfied than being married ten times.

He really had never courted a woman before... he prepares his ration and sets off to work in the early morning.

His footfalls down the protracted roads awaken the sun that announces the birth of a new scene... he never stopped even for moments to listen to the whispers of his colleagues in the weaving factory, relating their memories they had in the city... he has no memories to bring back, so why stop? Everything is going well with no one problem.

(2)

As unusual, it is a day of noise and clamor in the town... it is said that he is getting married... at last! His father decided to make a groom of him!

Some people are collecting some firewood and preparing the fireplace, some others are preparing the lunch; joy towers over everyone's face while some children are singing and dancing over the unpaved routes.

The well-wishers are flowing while the ceremony is not over yet... how tiring! He will have to shake hands with every one of them. He will have then to walk along with his friends down streets that he is not familiar with... he is fagged out... but... at last!...

He slowly walked with the door until it was closed shut, and then stuffed the ragged piece of cloth that his mother handed to him into the hole of the door.

He headed to her and slipped calmly to stick to her body when a tremor ran through his organs.

In spite of all the nights that he spent thinking about her and bringing her to his imagination, he still cannot draw her in clear lines.

She is, however, exactly as he imagined ... a white plump neck... long hair that enjoys playing with the white smooth back.

Out there, is still some murmuring as his family members and few of hers are waiting for the good news.

His hand mingles with her hair that is hanging down the breast and the shoulders, but no lust awakens! He, therefore, swoops down her lips in such a savage way... still nothing tasteful, but rather bitterness that brims his mouth:

What is that noxious red thing... he spits angrily on the floor..

He moves his hand to wipe that cylindrical twisted torso; it is not what he used to live with.

He fidgets for a while, looking round the room when suddenly an overwhelming delight descends upon him. It is the new furniture that flickers under the light of the oil lamp... his eyes stop at the wooden door to find the bolt unfastened.. he thinks for a while before he gets up to push it back with his hands... oh – how tired he is today... he leans on the edge of the bed, stoops down to untie the well-fastened laces of his shining black shoes. She, without being asked to, knows that she has to give him a wider room on the bed.

He opens wide his mouth giving a long but less foolish yawn... tosses to the right and starts to imagine... Harmonious full breasts ... round black eyes ... and a hot cylindrical torso... while the noise out becomes louder and louder...

Ink

(A writer open to his text)

He came to the whiteness of the paper without even a permission, and I, in turn, didn't ask him if something was to make him stay long or that he was just leaving...

He threw his flimsy body over the first line resting his waste leaching elbow over the top of the margin... there was a bad smell coming out of his pale black socks... he must have walked long before he decided to visit me...

- No greeting word? He said ironically.

- It is rather a wisp of farewell words or that of an impolite dismissal if you wish. I answered severely.

- Aha... ok ... I will overlook your being rude once again... I got wind of your determination to write me?

- You got wind!... I have just decided that when I was alone. What angel might have hurried to tell you so?

- Leave out the silly questions of yours. You know I live everywhere you do... in the house, the street, over your wife's bed ... I am all the time with you even when you are passing the waste of your full bowels into the toilet.

I hold the pen up to stab him in the head:

- Fie on you. How impudent!

He smiles satirically:

- What made you go mad? The cold wide bed of your wife? Or your full bowels with me watching your fragile waste?

- Your unwelcomed visit is what bothers me. I swear if you don't get away, I will cross you out with a stroke.

- I bet you can't. For it is so foolish to kill your hero from the very beginning.

- Ok now... what can I do for you to put an end to this vexing game?

- I want to stand as a witness on your story.

- A witness or a supervisor?

- Maybe both... come on give an ear to the neigh of the ink in your language, ride on your pen and thrust your spear in the breast of speech... tell your story with me for without me you might never be able to tell.

I belch ink out of my bowels and blow it into the quill and then arrange the papers vertically to cross the edge of the table:

- You can take a small step back to avoid the ink.

- Don't worry! I will not go to bed before I wash myself out from you papers.

- Back to being silly... who do you think you are to mock me like this?

- Don't waste time with such naïve quarrel... go ahead, I am helping you. How do you like to star? With a verb? Or maybe with a preposition.

- No! I will start with your name... Adam: "A" for all the depression that swallows the clouds before they rain, "D" for a necklace of flowers that you presented to your wife when hanger went to bed with both of you in the last hours of the night while you just kept silent. As for the "m", it is for your lovely dumb little daughter in whose eyes the vast universe of defeat dwells.

Yes, dear sirs, this is Adam, a story as big as its illusion. Away from the city, close to fear, he stands. He holds a hand back from prayer and raises the other to pray aloud (more joy O God... more joy).

- You make your guess just like this? Without even asking! Who told you my name is Adam?

- The apples your wife likes.

- So whoever has a wife who likes apples must be Adam, huh?... this is nonsense. It is a forgery!

- What is your name then?

- I don't recognize it very well, all I can remember is that I lost my identity in the very ancient wars. I was then working for the United Nations as a supervisor when some men arrested me. I no longer remember who they were fighting for. Anyway, they held me as a hostage and they demanded a ransom of two million dollars, or else , they said, they would trespass on the Mercedes cars all over Germany and, moreover, they would damage the outlets of the company.

- You must be hallucinating!

- No... I just have a confused memory.

- Then stop these bad interruptions. You are spoiling the story... who were we talking about?

- About ... my wife?

- Yeah... as sweet as sugar... redolent with the smell of Jasmine.. her warm bed sends forth, with the first breezes of the morning, a wild desire for the eternal death over the bed sheets of night... her white breasts are wo....

- No, no! This is too much. How dare you! She is my wife.

- Shut up. Or else, I will imprison you beyond the margins.

- You are a dictator.

- It is my paper

- And I am your hero

- Bakers never ask bread what kind of taste they wish to have. Nor do they ask them about the color.

- Fie on your vile lines... I do swear that any other criminal would have more just and mercy than you do if he were to write my story.

- Here I am. A writer so professional in humiliation. If you are well prepared for further scandals, you can go on with me, or you can leave me alone to manage to complete my story.

- Don't use that sense of possession. It is me who you are writing... what a bad encounter... you are fighting a poor disarmed man and vying with a hero of paper!

- I will keep silent, yes, I will do. But know this, you will regret. And you sleazy lines, lie down disappointed and wronged with a fighter who knocks out his fatigued heroes one after another to live alone in the middle of the page without a story.

- Nay, I will sure get out with my blue tattled paper while you finish your story to become among the masterpieces of art. The directors will haste from every corner of the Earth to bargain for it. Then I would answer them in a bit of a show-off language: (Hey traders, get away from my papers, my heroes are not for sale). Newspapers' headlines would be praising me and describing me as an ascetic.

- You will but one of the traders; you will be working against a principle you always boast of.

- How?

- Aren't you bartering something for another? Your glory for my scandal… your name with my being betrayed?

- Go away now… it is fruitless to go on with such a barren controversy… An idea is bombing hard my skull like a raid… I feel like a violent vertigo

as if an old oak tree is shaking inside my head...
Here it is... go back to your lines.

Here is your wife in the ninety-ninth night of your marriage... heavy rain hitting against the window and the meow of a lost cat brings you sleeplessness. You come closer to her body seeking some warmth, but she turns her back in a cold way that bitterly draws your ire... you remove the threadbare pillow away from her head and shout:

(I am cold)

She answers with a neutral voice that makes you burst of rage:

(I am hungry)

(Do not say apples again)

(Verily it is apples)

With an out-of-well movement, that you have thousands of times repeated, you get up to the clothes rail to put off your speckled nightshirt that was once your father's, and begin to button your coat.

It is one a.m. ... what street might snuggle you in such darkness, and what morning will you wait to fulfill her eternal desire.

Once again, five apples in a sack and one in your hand... you know well that they are not all yours... one is Newton's... another for Picasso... a third one is for the mud of the street.

This is the second street of the first avenue... walking that late here might make a suspicious of you.

How about taking you to another street? ... It is a bit longer but much safer.

- You are seeking my opinion! What a bastard! ... you decide on my name and destroy the last fence of mine, you then ask me about a way that I know you will choose whatever my desire be. You are such an impostor.

Then you shoot the apple of the mud at me, and I duck my head down

- What way did it go... I can hear it strike against the iron... how stupid! You hit that stately black car... look at those people coming out of the guarding cabin ... calm down... No, don't run they are running behind you... stop... NO... they will shoot... O Lord of honor and power... extend your aid to me to save him... six shots and the seventh makes you stumble and fall on the ground... don't look at me like this... hey

Adam I swear it is not me who did this, they are not in my story.

- This makes no difference, I am dying.

- But where did they come from?

- Maybe from a neighboring story.

- That is not possible, I have already brought my papers into ashes and blew them away over the graves of the desert.

- Oh... I feel pain... I want to howl like a she-wolf, to cry like a bereaved mother, to out laugh like a prostitute. Somebody help me, come on, don't just watch me, any verb of a survival meaning might help me

- Oh God! What verb? live... survive... or maybe overcome... yes that's it. I hurry to write (Adam overcomes death and stands on his feet)

- Somewhere to hide, quickly please!

(Adam will seek the nearest darkness)

- They are shooting again Adam, get down... a bullet in your head... another in your breast... Stop you bastards, damn you! Who on earth allowed you in my story? Get out... you are staining my papers with blood... you are wounding the lines with your boots... you there!

The ever lurking behind the lines… come to fight me pen to rifle …

There is more of them Adam… I can hear the hissing of their feet over the words… Oh God! Whose are all those rifles?

Here they are spreading over the whole page, shooting at me… a shot, two, three… a hundred, and I fall over your corpse with my head and pen bleeding.